# FIND YOUR PARK!
## NATIONAL PARKS STAMPBOOK
## FOR
## KIDS

*Attach an image of yourself when starting the book here!*

This book belongs to:

_____

Age at start:_____

Date the adventure began:

_____

# DEDICATION

This National Parks Notebook is dedicated to all the National Park Lovers out there who love to plan out and visit the state parks, and document their findings in the process.

You are my inspiration for producing books and I'm honored to be a part of keeping all of your notes and records organized.

# How to use this National Parks Stamp Notebook:

This useful national parks project log book is a must-have for anyone that loves the art of travel and visiting the national state parks! You will love this easy to use journal to track and record all your national park activities.

Each interior page includes space to record & track the following:

Visit Date - Write down the date of the current park project.
Number of Days At The Park - Use this space to fill in the number of days you were theret.
Your Reflections On The Park - Record any thoughts, observations of this park.
Stamp or Sticker - Fill in the stamp or sticker in this space.

If you are new to the world of traveling to visit the national parks or have been at it for a while, this national park stamp book organizer is a must have! Can make a great useful gift for anyone that loves to visit the national state parks!

Have Fun!

# reflection | noun | re·flec·tion

consideration of some subject matter, idea, or purpose

Take some time to reflect as you complete this book and your visit to the National Parks. Why are our National Parks important? What does this park, or this spot in the park mean to you? How will you help protect this park and our national resources?

# Acadia National Park

Location: Maine

Year established: 1919

Visit Date:_____

Number of days at the park: _____

Your reflections on the park: _____

_____

_____

_____

```
                    Stamp Here
```

# N.P. of American Samoa

Location: American Samoa
Year established: 1988
Visit Date:_____
Number of days at the park: _____
Your reflections on the park: _____
_____
_____
_____

```
┌─────────────────────────────────────┐
│                                     │
│                                     │
│                                     │
│             Stamp Here              │
│                                     │
│                                     │
│                                     │
└─────────────────────────────────────┘
```

# Arches National Park

Location: Utah

Year established: 1971

Visit Date:_____

Number of days at the park: _____

Your reflections on the park: _____

_____

_____

_____

Stamp Here

# Badlands National Park

Location: South Dakota
Year established: 1978
Visit Date:_____
Number of days at the park: _____
Your reflections on the park: _____
_____
_____
_____

Stamp Here

# Big Bend National Park

Location: Texas

Year established: 1974

Visit Date:_____

Number of days at the park: _____

Your reflections on the park: _____

_____

_____

_____

Stamp Here

# Biscayne National Park

Location: Florida

Year established: 1980

Visit Date:_____

Number of days at the park: _____

Your reflections on the park: _____

_____

_____

_____

*Stamp Here*

# Black Canyon - Gunnison

Location: Colorado

Year established: 1999

Visit Date:_____

Number of days at the park: _____

Your reflections on the park: _____

_____

_____

_____

*Stamp Here*

# Bryce Canyon N.P

Location: Utah
Year established: 1928
Visit Date:_____
Number of days at the park: _____
Your reflections on the park: _____
_____
_____
_____

Stamp Here

# Canyonlands N.P.

Location: Utah
Year established: 1964
Visit Date:_____
Number of days at the park: _____
Your reflections on the park: _____
_____
_____
_____

```
┌────────────────────────────────────────┐
│                                        │
│                                        │
│                                        │
│              Stamp Here                │
│                                        │
│                                        │
│                                        │
└────────────────────────────────────────┘
```

# Capital Reef N.P.

Location: Utah
Year established: 1971
Visit Date:_____
Number of days at the park: _____
Your reflections on the park: _____
_____
_____
_____

Stamp Here

# Carlsbad Caverns N.P.

Location: New Mexico
Year established: 1930
Visit Date:_____
Number of days at the park: _____
Your reflections on the park: _____
_____
_____
_____

Stamp Here

# Channel Islands N.P.

Location: California

Year established: 1980

Visit Date:_____

Number of days at the park: _____

Your reflections on the park: _____

_____

_____

_____

```
┌─────────────────────────────────────┐
│                                     │
│                                     │
│              Stamp Here              │
│                                     │
│                                     │
└─────────────────────────────────────┘
```

# Conagree National Park

Location: South Carolina

Year established: 2003

Visit Date:_____

Number of days at the park: _____

Your reflections on the park: _____

_____

_____

_____

Stamp Here

# Crater Lake N.P.

Location: Oregon
Year established: 1902
Visit Date:_____
Number of days at the park: _____
Your reflections on the park: _____
_____
_____
_____

Stamp Here

# Cuyahoga Valley N.P.

Location: Ohio
Year established: 2000
Visit Date:_____
Number of days at the park: _____
Your reflections on the park: _____
_____
_____
_____

Stamp Here

# Death Valley N.P.

Location: California, Nevada

Year established: 1994

Visit Date:_____

Number of days at the park: _____

Your reflections on the park: _____

_____

_____

_____

Stamp Here

# Denali National Park

Location: Alaska
Year established: 1917
Visit Date:_____
Number of days at the park: _____
Your reflections on the park: _____
_____
_____
_____

|  |
|---|
| Stamp Here |

# Dry Tortugas N.P.

Location: Florida
Year established: 1992
Visit Date:_____
Number of days at the park: _____
Your reflections on the park: _____
_____
_____
_____

Stamp Here

# Everglades N.P.

Location: Florida

Year established: 1934

Visit Date:_____

Number of days at the park: _____

Your reflections on the park: _____

_____

_____

_____

Stamp Here

# Gates of the Arctic N.P.

Location: Alaska
Year established: 1980
Visit Date:_____
Number of days at the park: _____
Your reflections on the park: _____
_____
_____
_____

Stamp Here

# Glacier National Park

Location: Montana
Year established: 1910
Visit Date:_____
Number of days at the park: _____
Your reflections on the park: _____
_____
_____
_____

Stamp Here

# Glacier Bay N.P.

Location: Alaska
Year established: 1980
Visit Date:_____
Number of days at the park: _____
Your reflections on the park: _____
_____
_____
_____

Stamp Here

# Grand Canyon N.P.

Location: Arizona

Year established: 1919

Visit Date:_____

Number of days at the park: _____

Your reflections on the park: _____

_____

_____

_____

Stamp Here

# Grand Teton N.P.

Location: Wyoming
Year established: 1929
Visit Date:_____
Number of days at the park: _____
Your reflections on the park: _____
_____
_____
_____

```
┌────────────────────────────────────────┐
│                                        │
│                                        │
│                                        │
│              Stamp Here                │
│                                        │
│                                        │
│                                        │
└────────────────────────────────────────┘
```

# Great Basin N.P.

Location: Nevada

Year established: 1986

Visit Date:_____

Number of days at the park: _____

Your reflections on the park: _____

_____

_____

_____

Stamp Here

# Great Sand Dunes N.P.

Location: Colorado
Year established: 2004
Visit Date:_____
Number of days at the park: _____
Your reflections on the park: _____
_____
_____
_____

Stamp Here

# Great Smoky Mtns. N.P.

Location: Tennessee, North Carolina

Year established: 1934

Visit Date:_____

Number of days at the park: _____

Your reflections on the park: _____

_____

_____

_____

Stamp Here

# Guadalupe N.P.

Location: Texas
Year established: 1966
Visit Date:_____
Number of days at the park: _____
Your reflections on the park: _____
_____
_____
_____

Stamp Here

# Haleakalā National Park

Location: Hawai'i
Year established: 1916
Visit Date:_____
Number of days at the park: _____
Your reflections on the park: _____
_____
_____
_____

Stamp Here

# Hawai'i Volcanoes N.P.

Location: Hawai'i
Year established: 1916
Visit Date:_____
Number of days at the park: _____
Your reflections on the park: _____
_____
_____
_____

Stamp Here

# Hot Springs N.P.

Location: Arkansas
Year established: 1921
Visit Date:_____
Number of days at the park: _____
Your reflections on the park: _____
_____
_____
_____

Stamp Here

# Isle Royale N.P.

Location: Michigan
Year established: 1940
Visit Date:_____
Number of days at the park: _____
Your reflections on the park: _____
_____
_____
_____

```
                        Stamp Here
```

# Joshua Tree N.P.

Location: California

Year established: 1994

Visit Date:_____

Number of days at the park: _____

Your reflections on the park: _____

_____

_____

_____

Stamp Here

# Katmai National Park

Location: Alaska
Year established: 1980
Visit Date:_____
Number of days at the park: _____
Your reflections on the park: _____
_____
_____
_____

```
┌─────────────────────────────────────┐
│                                     │
│                                     │
│                                     │
│             Stamp Here              │
│                                     │
│                                     │
│                                     │
└─────────────────────────────────────┘
```

# Kenai Fjords N.P.

Location: Alaska
Year established: 1980
Visit Date:_____
Number of days at the park: _____
Your reflections on the park: _____
_____
_____
_____

Stamp Here

# Kings Canyon N.P.

Location: California
Year established: 1940
Visit Date:_____
Number of days at the park: _____
Your reflections on the park: _____
_____
_____
_____

Stamp Here

# Kobuk Valley N.P.

Location: Alaska

Year established: 1980

Visit Date:_____

Number of days at the park: _____

Your reflections on the park: _____

_____

_____

_____

Stamp Here

# Lake Clark N.P.

Location: Alaska
Year established: 1980
Visit Date:_____
Number of days at the park: _____
Your reflections on the park: _____
_____
_____
_____

Stamp Here

# Lassen Volcanic N.P.

Location: California

Year established: 1916

Visit Date:_____

Number of days at the park: _____

Your reflections on the park: _____

_____

_____

_____

Stamp Here

# Mammoth Cave N.P.

Location: Kentucky

Year established: 1941

Visit Date:_____

Number of days at the park: _____

Your reflections on the park: _____

_____

_____

_____

```
┌──────────────────────────────────────┐
│                                      │
│                                      │
│              Stamp Here              │
│                                      │
│                                      │
└──────────────────────────────────────┘
```

# Mesa Verde N.P.

Location: Colorado

Year established: 1906

Visit Date:_____

Number of days at the park: _____

Your reflections on the park: _____

_____

_____

_____

Stamp Here

# Mount Rainier N.P.

Location: Washington
Year established: 1899
Visit Date:_____
Number of days at the park: _____
Your reflections on the park: _____
_____
_____
_____

Stamp Here

# North Cascades N.P.

Location: Washington
Year established: 1968
Visit Date:_____
Number of days at the park: _____
Your reflections on the park: _____
_____
_____
_____

Stamp Here

# Olympic National Park

Location: Washington
Year established: 1938
Visit Date:_____
Number of days at the park: _____
Your reflections on the park: _____
_____
_____
_____

```
                  Stamp Here
```

# Petrified Forest N.P.

Location: Arizona

Year established: 1962

Visit Date:_____

Number of days at the park: _____

Your reflections on the park: _____

_____

_____

_____

Stamp Here

# Pinnacles National Park

Location: California
Year established: 2013
Visit Date:_____
Number of days at the park: _____
Your reflections on the park: _____
_____
_____
_____

```
┌─────────────────────────────────────┐
│                                     │
│                                     │
│                                     │
│                                     │
│             Stamp Here              │
│                                     │
│                                     │
│                                     │
│                                     │
└─────────────────────────────────────┘
```

# Redwood National Park

Location: California

Year established: 1968

Visit Date:_____

Number of days at the park: _____

Your reflections on the park: _____

_____

_____

_____

Stamp Here

# Rocky Mountain N.P.

Location: Colorado
Year established: 1915
Visit Date:_____
Number of days at the park: _____
Your reflections on the park: _____
_____
_____
_____

Stamp Here

# Saguaro National Park

Location: Arizona
Year established: 1994
Visit Date:_____
Number of days at the park: _____
Your reflections on the park: _____
_____
_____
_____

Stamp Here

# Sequoia National Park

Location: California

Year established: 1890

Visit Date:_____

Number of days at the park: _____

Your reflections on the park: _____

_____

_____

_____

```
┌─────────────────────────────────────┐
│                                     │
│                                     │
│                                     │
│                                     │
│            Stamp Here               │
│                                     │
│                                     │
│                                     │
│                                     │
└─────────────────────────────────────┘
```

# Shenandoah N.P.

Location: Virginia

Year established: 1935

Visit Date:_____

Number of days at the park: _____

Your reflections on the park: _____

_____

_____

_____

Stamp Here

# Theodore Roosevelt N.P.

Location: North Dakota
Year established: 1978
Visit Date:_____
Number of days at the park: _____
Your reflections on the park: _____
_____
_____
_____

Stamp Here

# Virgin Islands N.P.

Location: U.S. Virgin Islands
Year established: 1956
Visit Date:_____
Number of days at the park: _____
Your reflections on the park: _____
_____
_____
_____

Stamp Here

# Voyageurs N.P.

Location: Minnesota
Year established: 1971
Visit Date:_____
Number of days at the park: _____
Your reflections on the park: _____
_____
_____
_____

```
                    Stamp Here
```

# Wind Cave N.P.

Location: South Dakota
Year established: 1903
Visit Date:_____
Number of days at the park: _____
Your reflections on the park: _____
_____
_____
_____

Stamp Here

# Wrangell-St. Elias N.P.

Location: Alaska
Year established: 1980
Visit Date:_____
Number of days at the park: _____
Your reflections on the park: _____
_____
_____
_____

Stamp Here

# Yellowstone N.P.

Location: Wyoming, Montana, Idaho
Year established: 1872
Visit Date:_____
Number of days at the park: _____
Your reflections on the park: _____
_____
_____
_____

Stamp Here

# Yosemite National Park

Location: California
Year established: 1890
Visit Date:_____
Number of days at the park: _____
Your reflections on the park: _____
_____
_____
_____

Stamp Here

# Zion National Park

Location: Utah

Year established: 1919

Visit Date:_____

Number of days at the park: _____

Your reflections on the park: _____

_____

_____

_____

Stamp Here

# Acadia National Park

Location: Maine
Year established: 1919
Visit Date:_____
Number of days at the park: _____
Your reflections on the park: _____
_____
_____
_____

Stamp Here

# N.P. of American Samoa

Location: American Samoa

Year established: 1988

Visit Date:_____

Number of days at the park: _____

Your reflections on the park: _____

_____

_____

_____

```
┌────────────────────────────────────────┐
│                                        │
│                                        │
│                                        │
│              Stamp Here                │
│                                        │
│                                        │
│                                        │
└────────────────────────────────────────┘
```

# Arches National Park

Location: Utah

Year established: 1971

Visit Date:_____

Number of days at the park: _____

Your reflections on the park: _____

_____

_____

_____

Stamp Here

# Badlands National Park

Location: South Dakota

Year established: 1978

Visit Date:_____

Number of days at the park: _____

Your reflections on the park: _____

_____

_____

_____

Stamp Here

# Big Bend National Park

Location: Texas

Year established: 1974

Visit Date:_____

Number of days at the park: _____

Your reflections on the park: _____

_____

_____

_____

Stamp Here

# Biscayne National Park

Location: Florida

Year established: 1980

Visit Date:_____

Number of days at the park: _____

Your reflections on the park: _____

_____

_____

_____

# Black Canyon - Gunnison

Location: Colorado
Year established: 1999
Visit Date:_____
Number of days at the park: _____
Your reflections on the park: _____
_____
_____
_____

Stamp Here

# Bryce Canyon N.P

Location: Utah
Year established: 1928
Visit Date:_____
Number of days at the park: _____
Your reflections on the park: _____
_____
_____
_____

Stamp Here

# Canyonlands N.P.

Location: Utah

Year established: 1964

Visit Date:_____

Number of days at the park: _____

Your reflections on the park: _____

_____

_____

_____

Stamp Here

# Capital Reef N.P.

Location: Utah

Year established: 1971

Visit Date:_____

Number of days at the park: _____

Your reflections on the park: _____

_____

_____

_____

Stamp Here

# Carlsbad Caverns N.P.

Location: New Mexico
Year established: 1930
Visit Date:_____
Number of days at the park: _____
Your reflections on the park: _____
_____
_____
_____

Stamp Here

# Channel Islands N.P.

Location: California
Year established: 1980
Visit Date:_____
Number of days at the park: _____
Your reflections on the park: _____
_____
_____
_____

[ Stamp Here ]

# Conagree National Park

Location: South Carolina
Year established: 2003
Visit Date:_____
Number of days at the park: _____
Your reflections on the park: _____
_____
_____
_____

Stamp Here

# Crater Lake N.P.

Location: Oregon
Year established: 1902
Visit Date:_____
Number of days at the park: _____
Your reflections on the park: _____
_____
_____
_____

```
┌──────────────────────────────────────┐
│                                      │
│                                      │
│                                      │
│             Stamp Here               │
│                                      │
│                                      │
│                                      │
└──────────────────────────────────────┘
```

# Cuyahoga Valley N.P.

Location: Ohio
Year established: 2000
Visit Date:_____
Number of days at the park: _____
Your reflections on the park: _____
_____
_____
_____

```
                   Stamp Here
```

# Death Valley N.P.

Location: California, Nevada
Year established: 1994
Visit Date:_____
Number of days at the park: _____
Your reflections on the park: _____
_____
_____
_____

Stamp Here

# Denali National Park

Location: Alaska
Year established: 1917
Visit Date:_____
Number of days at the park: _____
Your reflections on the park: _____
_____
_____
_____

Stamp Here

# Dry Tortugas N.P.

Location: Florida
Year established: 1992
Visit Date:_____
Number of days at the park: _____
Your reflections on the park: _____
_____
_____
_____

Stamp Here

# Everglades N.P.

Location: Florida
Year established: 1934
Visit Date:_____
Number of days at the park: _____
Your reflections on the park: _____
_____
_____
_____

Stamp Here

# Gates of the Arctic N.P.

Location: Alaska
Year established: 1980
Visit Date:_____
Number of days at the park: _____
Your reflections on the park: _____
_____
_____
_____

Stamp Here

# Glacier National Park

Location: Montana
Year established: 1910
Visit Date:_____
Number of days at the park: _____
Your reflections on the park: _____
_____
_____
_____

Stamp Here

# Glacier Bay N.P.

Location: Alaska

Year established: 1980

Visit Date:_____

Number of days at the park: _____

Your reflections on the park: _____

_____

_____

_____

Stamp Here

# Grand Canyon N.P.

Location: Arizona
Year established: 1919
Visit Date:_____
Number of days at the park: _____
Your reflections on the park: _____
_____
_____
_____

Stamp Here

# Grand Teton N.P.

Location: Wyoming
Year established: 1929
Visit Date:_____
Number of days at the park: _____
Your reflections on the park: _____
_____
_____
_____

Stamp Here

# Great Basin N.P.

Location: Nevada
Year established: 1986
Visit Date:_____
Number of days at the park: _____
Your reflections on the park: _____
_____
_____
_____

Stamp Here

# Great Sand Dunes N.P.

Location: Colorado
Year established: 2004
Visit Date:_____
Number of days at the park: _____
Your reflections on the park: _____
_____
_____
_____

Stamp Here

# Great Smoky Mtns. N.P.

Location: Tennessee, North Carolina
Year established: 1934
Visit Date: _____
Number of days at the park: _____
Your reflections on the park: _____
_____
_____
_____

Stamp Here

# Guadalupe N.P.

Location: Texas
Year established: 1966
Visit Date:_____
Number of days at the park: _____
Your reflections on the park: _____
_____
_____
_____

Stamp Here

# Haleakalā National Park

Location: Hawai'i

Year established: 1916

Visit Date:_____

Number of days at the park: _____

Your reflections on the park: _____

_____

_____

_____

```
┌────────────────────────────────────────┐
│                                        │
│                                        │
│                                        │
│              Stamp Here                │
│                                        │
│                                        │
│                                        │
└────────────────────────────────────────┘
```

# Hawai'i Volcanoes N.P.

Location: Hawai'i

Year established: 1916

Visit Date:_____

Number of days at the park: _____

Your reflections on the park: _____

_____

_____

_____

```
┌──────────────────────────────────────┐
│                                      │
│                                      │
│                                      │
│                                      │
│             Stamp Here               │
│                                      │
│                                      │
│                                      │
│                                      │
└──────────────────────────────────────┘
```

# Hot Springs N.P.

Location: Arkansas
Year established: 1921
Visit Date:_____
Number of days at the park: _____
Your reflections on the park: _____
_____
_____
_____

```
                    Stamp Here
```

# Isle Royale N.P.

Location: Michigan
Year established: 1940
Visit Date:_____
Number of days at the park: _____
Your reflections on the park: _____
_____
_____
_____

Stamp Here

# Joshua Tree N.P.

Location: California
Year established: 1994
Visit Date:_____
Number of days at the park: _____
Your reflections on the park: _____
_____
_____
_____

Stamp Here

# Katmai National Park

Location: Alaska
Year established: 1980
Visit Date:_____
Number of days at the park: _____
Your reflections on the park: _____
_____
_____
_____

Stamp Here

# Kenai Fjords N.P.

Location: Alaska
Year established: 1980
Visit Date:_____
Number of days at the park: _____
Your reflections on the park: _____
_____
_____
_____

```
                    Stamp Here
```

# Kings Canyon N.P.

Location: California

Year established: 1940

Visit Date:_____

Number of days at the park: _____

Your reflections on the park: _____

_____

_____

_____

*Stamp Here*

# Kobuk Valley N.P.

Location: Alaska
Year established: 1980
Visit Date:_____
Number of days at the park: _____
Your reflections on the park: _____
_____
_____
_____

Stamp Here

# Lake Clark N.P.

Location: Alaska
Year established: 1980
Visit Date:_____
Number of days at the park: _____
Your reflections on the park: _____
_____
_____
_____

Stamp Here

# Lassen Volcanic N.P.

Location: California
Year established: 1916
Visit Date:_____
Number of days at the park: _____
Your reflections on the park: _____
_____
_____
_____

|  |
|---|
| Stamp Here |

# Mammoth Cave N.P.

Location: Kentucky

Year established: 1941

Visit Date:_____

Number of days at the park: _____

Your reflections on the park: _____

_____

_____

_____

Stamp Here

# Mesa Verde N.P.

Location: Colorado
Year established: 1906
Visit Date:_____
Number of days at the park: _____
Your reflections on the park: _____
_____
_____
_____

Stamp Here

# Mount Rainier N.P.

Location: Washington

Year established: 1899

Visit Date:_____

Number of days at the park: _____

Your reflections on the park: _____

_____

_____

_____

Stamp Here

# North Cascades N.P.

Location: Washington
Year established: 1968
Visit Date:_____
Number of days at the park: _____
Your reflections on the park: _____
_____
_____
_____

Stamp Here

# Olympic National Park

Location: Washington
Year established: 1938
Visit Date:_____
Number of days at the park: _____
Your reflections on the park: _____
_____
_____
_____

Stamp Here

# Petrified Forest N.P.

Location: Arizona
Year established: 1962
Visit Date:_____
Number of days at the park: _____
Your reflections on the park: _____
_____
_____
_____

Stamp Here

# Pinnacles National Park

Location: California

Year established: 2013

Visit Date:_____

Number of days at the park: _____

Your reflections on the park: _____

_____

_____

_____

Stamp Here

www.ingramcontent.com/pod-product-compliance
Lightning Source LLC
Chambersburg PA
CBHW080215040426
42333CB00044B/2699